OLE G. JENSEN

C000212575

THE CULTURE OF GREENLAND IN GLIMPSES

milik publishing

Hans Knutsen/ © Arktisk Institut

CONTENTS

FOREWORD

This book, which is about parts of the spiritual and material cultural inheritance of Greenland, gives us a long-awaited, easily-accessible, short and animated description of many of the phenomena upon which Greenland's culture is built. Hopefully, many people will enjoy the book, in particular visitors to Greenland who are looking for a short introduction to those parts of Greenland's culture that are only heard of sporadically.

Greenland's cultural inheritance, with its origins in Inuit cultures, is well-represented in the literature, but often in a form that is not easily accessible. This book provides a fine insight into the mindset that existed amongst the ancestors of present-day Greenlanders and on which some present day art and culture is based. I hope only that the book may provide constant inspiration for others who are interested in the cultural inheritance of the Inuit. There is still much to be drawn from the culture and traditions of the Inuit, even in today's globalized world.

Daniel Thorleifsen
Leader
The National Museum of Greenland

Hans Knutsen/ © Arktisk Institut

TUPILAK

The tupilak, the world-famous figure, was originally feared and hated. In it's present shape, it is valued by collectors of Inuit art, and by tourists to Greenland as an ordinary souvenir.

The word *tupilak* describes a wide variety of small figures which represent either tupilaks or other mythical and spiritual creatures, and it can be difficult to see the difference. Originally the tupilak was a creature composed of different materials from the natural world – animal, bird, or human remains – even parts taken from a child's corpse. The shaman, knowledgeable about witchcraft, would gather bits and pieces at a secret, isolated place, tie them together, chant magic spells over the tied up bundle, and then allow the tied up bits and pieces to draw sexual energy from the shaman's own genitalia.

The tupilak was then ready to

F.C.P. Rüttel/ © Arktisk Institut

5

be put into the sea and sent off to kill an enemy. This way of getting rid of your enemies was, however, not entirely without risk because if the would-be victim had greater powers of wizardry than the initiator, his power could return the tupilak's strength and potency like a boomerang. In other words, it was a dangerous game – a Greenlandic version of Russian roulette.

No original tupilaks remain. They have vanished from the scene because they were made of perishable materials. They were, for good reason, "disposable" tupilaks and were not meant to be seen by others.

When curious ignorant Europeans came to Greenland, figures were carved to show the visitors what the creature looked like. The tupilak figure is known throughout all of the Eskimo regions. Throughout time, tupilak figures have been carved in different materials all over Greenland. The oldest known tupilaks are made of wood with a skin belt and they resemble the authentic ancient figures. Today these carvings are associated with East Greenland, the old traditions being more alive there as that culture has always maintained a rich carving tradition.

The more grotesque and terrifying the figure, the easier it was to sell. It became quite an industry for especially East Greenlandic artists who made tupilaks in the form most of us are familiar with today.

From the 1950s up until the 1970s, large numbers of these figures were produced in a more or less stereotypical form, although now and again the

artists created figures of great artistic craftsmanship. Today the figures are still produced, but due to whale conservation, they are usually made from reindeer horn or narwhal tusk.

Contemporary tupilaks are not dangerous. The only risk you take is that you might become fascinated by Greenlandic mythology. But most of us can live with that…

F.C.P. Rüttel/ © Arktisk Institut

MASKS

When you put on a mask, your identity changes and suddenly you are free to step out of your usual role and behave like another being or person. The mask is a means of concealing your true identity from your neighbours or from spirits and other higher powers.

The mask is known in all cultures and used in many contexts – in cults or in more earthbound connection for pure entertainment.

Greenlandic masks are known primarily from East Greenland which can be described as having a genuine mask culture. Only a few examples of masks can be found in West Greenland and here the artistic expression is totally different.

Not much is known about the role of masks in traditional societies and not many masks exist prior to the turn of the 20th century. The reason may lie in the mask's strong personal link with its owner. Masks have often followed their owners to the grave or perhaps been destroyed by death. Another

9

theory is that the mask's power was so great that it had to be destroyed after use in a cult context.

East Greenlandic masks are often described as *dancing masks* to be used in connection with different kinds of ceremonies or lamp extinguishing games. *Theatrical masks* were used for entertainment and *house masks*, which were smaller than the others, represented a domestic spirit and protected the home and its members.

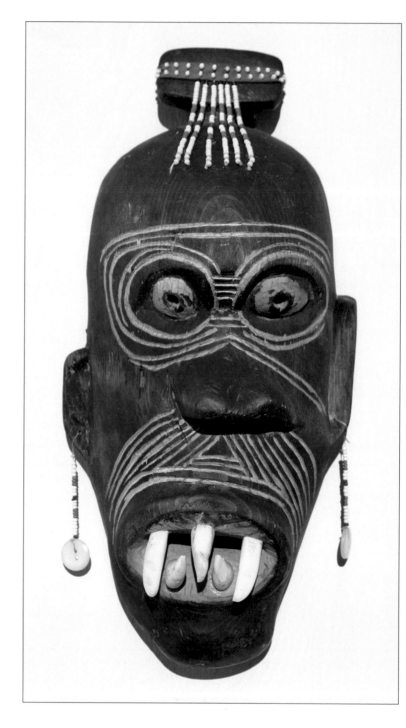

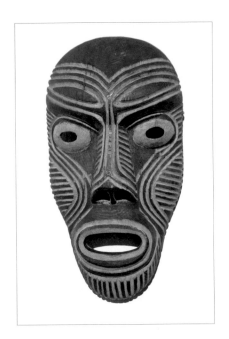 

Masks were often decorated, even if only modestly in comparison with masks from Canada and Alaska. Usually lines or skeleton ornamentation are carved into the wood. More rarely, bits of hide are present. Now and again teeth and pieces of hair and suchlike are inset.

Line ornamentation is also known in tattooing among the Inuit where it functions as a sort of special-occasion calendar marking e.g. a first birth, a boy's first seal kill, etc.

The colour of the mask is usually black and comes from lamp soot. On newer masks red can be seen.

The simplest mask is made by colouring the face black, whiting out a couple of lines and putting a stick in the mouth, thereby changing the facial expression completely. This mask tradition has been adopted extensively by contemporary Greenlandic actors.

Another mask tradition is the *mitaartut mask* which is traditionally made of skin. This tradition still survives in Greenland. At epiphany (January 6th) both children and adults visit neighbouring houses and demand whatever they want. They must be given what they ask for, although nowadays demands are limited to sweets, buns and loose change. The intention behind the masks has nothing to do with the world of spirits. They are just made to make the bearer unrecognizable. The mask material or its decoration may be of any kind of second-hand materials and ideas are abundant.

After the introduction of Christianity, the purpose of the mask was reduced to frightening children when they needed a bit of discipline. Later it became a simple tourist souvenir. Where the old masks could express both sexes in one mask, masks are now produced in pairs.

Masks, including Eskimo masks, have been a source of inspiration throughout this century to artists worldwide such as Matisse, Picasso and many others.

AMULETS

Hans Knutsen/ © Arktisk Institut

During the last part of his voyage from Greenland to the Pacific in 1924, Knud Rasmussen interviewed the shaman Najagneqey in Nome, Alaska.

Knud Rasmussen asked: – What is your impression of the way people live? Najagneq answered: – They are at odds with themselves, because they mix everything together and weak, because they can no longer do one thing at a time. A great hunter must not at the same time be a great lover of women. But no-one is able to stop.

– Animals are inscrutable. So he, who lives off them, must be careful. But people arm themselves with amulets and are alone in their decrepitude.

– There must be as many different amulets as possible in a settlement. Similarity splits the power, likeness makes worthless.

These are strong words from an old shaman. The rest of us can understand the need of the Arctic peoples to seek

protection against constantly lurking dangers and the ever-present threat of death. If there was help in an amulet, then it must be tried.

The use of amulets was widespread throughout the entire Eskimo region, including Greenland. Just about anything could be used as an amulet. Amulets were not necessarily beautiful, valuable or rare things. They were objects recommended by others in the settlement as being especially useful in a given situation. Bits of wood, feathers, something from an animal, stones, beads, even dirt was

mentioned as a possible ingredient in an amulet. An infinite number of things could be used.

The amulets were worn on the body, either sewn into a strap or into clothing. Other amulets could have their own special place in the skin tent, the kayak or the umiaq.

Amulets were used by men, women and children for a long life, good hunting and safety at sea, against sickness and its after-effects, but could also be used by mothers to ensure their children a good life, with

good hunting, luck with a harpoon and much more. The amulets were always carefully looked after and they were well hidden. An amulet was a very secret and personal thing.

Knud Rasmussen mentions an expression of parental love shown by the Netsilik people of Canada. Here he met a seven-year old boy with more than 80 amulets sewn into his clothing. The boy's play was somewhat inhibited by such concern for his well-being.

The symbolism of an amulet and its assumed effects is usually very direct, as an old East Greenlander explains: – You find an Arctic willow that grows straight up and you carve a doll from the thickest part of the stem. You tie the doll under the hat of a boy.

– For the willows that grow straight up have a

stronger vitality than those that creep along the ground and such an amulet not only makes the boy grow quickly, but he will also have a strong back and he will be able to go through life without being afraid of anything.

The security and strength of an amulet can also be recognized in present day life. We call it something else, but many people have a lucky coin or some other small thing in their pocket or purse.

Most visitors to Greenland take home a necklace or some other piece of handicraft, such as a little carving of a polar bear head or claw.

Even though the handicraft is mainly a lovely souvenir of Greenland, it just might also impart a little of the bear's strength!

THE INUIT DRUM

The drum has been known and used throughout the entire Arctic region. It represents a tradition that has been adapted to the special nomadic way of life of the Inuit and which has made a great impact on their culture and society. The unwritten history of the Inuit has survived in songs, stories and legends passed on from one generation to the next on dark winter evenings, accompanied by the monotonous rhythm of the drum.

The main variations in the appearance of the drum are its size – from about 1 meter in diameter in Western Canada and Alaska to the small drum we know from the polar Eskimos of the Thule region. Its general shape is a more or less round ring with a small handle, often decorated with a little carved face. Preferably, the ring should be covered with skin from the stomach of a bear or walrus, but other animal skins have been used.

The availability of wood in the area determined the size of the drum. Polar Eskimos often made the ring by joining pieces of bone or reindeer antler and this put a limit on the size of the diameter.

The last part of the drum set is the drumstick, which in Greenland is used to beat the edge of the drum, on the wooden or bone rim. The drumstick is made of wood. It is a little longer than the diameter of the drum and is sometimes decorated with a simple carving. There should be no knots in the wood, as these were believed to be spiritual power points of the forefathers. It was therefore considered unfair in a song fight to use a drumstick with knots.

The drum dance or drum song was an event that took place both in summer and winter and could be performed by both men and women. The songs can be divided into many groups, each with its own social function. Some of the more important functions are described below.

The drum dance as a court of law – the song duel – where disputes were settled usually took place at summer gatherings. The "winner" of such a duel was the person who received most applause and made the audience laugh the most. The loser could get revenge at a new song duel at a later time.

The Shaman's use of the drum to cast spells and communicate with the spirits was a part of the drum ceremony that greatly disturbed the missionaries, so it was promptly forbidden.

The drum could also be used for pure entertainment. It was used to accompany stories of the past and songs for children at festivals. In East Greenland in particular the drum was a source of entertainment and since the missionaries didn't arrive here until just over a hundred years ago, many of the songs from this area have been preserved.

Nowadays, the drum songs are generally performed for the sake of tourists and entertainment, but they are still treated with respect. There are still songs that are not sung just for anyone, anywhere, at any time. Even in a modern world, where the drum skin might be made out of the remains of a weather balloon, some mysticism lingers on.

A drum hangs in most courtrooms in Greenland – a

symbol of settling disputes. The National Library in Greenland has a drum dancer in its logo, signifying the power of legends and story telling.

The culture centre in Nuuk, Katuaq, is named after the drumstick. There is a lot of symbolism here, especially if the drumstick is made of very knotty wood!

Th. Krabbe/ © Arktisk Institut

THE SHAMAN

Everything has life. And this is not only true of the world we see. Countless spirits occupy the air, the ground, the sea and remote areas far from human habitation. Some are friendly, most are hostile and all are more or less unpredictable. Anybody who does not understand how to stay friends with them risks their wrath. But that is not all. A mysterious power pervades and fills our entire existence.

It was difficult for an ordinary person to hold his own in such an incomprehensible and dangerous world as this. But in olden times, it was part of the every-day life of the Inuit and it explains the importance of the role played by the shaman, medicine man or angakkoq (Greenlandic version).

When you feared evil, it was essential to be on good terms with these inexplicable, hidden and unpredictable forces. It was important not to offend life, prey or nature. As a consequence, rituals and taboos must be followed unconditionally so as not to disturb the equilibrium – the balance of nature. And the shaman – male or female – was the link that ensured that things were done the right way.

It was often sickness or bad hunting that made it necessary to commune with the spirit world. The mother of the sea, the moon man and the entrails-seizer are some of the more familiar, powerful spirit beings and it required great courage to stand up to these great spirits so the settlement could have hap-

pier days. It was the angakkoq's responsibility to take dangerous journeys to pacify these beings.

Shaman training took a long time and it was difficult and dangerous. The training consisted of a practical part and a theoretical part and usually started in childhood.

The teacher had to be an older, experienced shaman. It was often the young men who, either of their own accord or after being pointed out by family or neighbours, became apprentice angakkoqs. Some sources suggest a training period of 3-4 years, others up to 12 years.

The theoretical part consisted of acquiring knowledge of ordinary shaman techniques, the invisible world and learning about myths and legends retold by an experienced shaman.

The practical part had to take place in secrecy out of consideration for the others in the community. One of the purposes of this part was to get hold of as many helping spirits as possible.

An important element was the death-rebirth experience. What usually happened, was that the apprentice sought a place of solitude and found a rubbing stone – a smooth stone which he rubbed

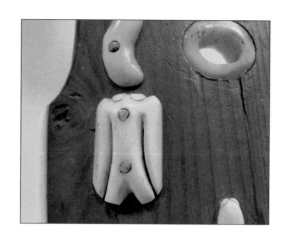

monotonously in circles on a flat rock until he either went into a trance or lost consciousness. Whilst in this state, the apprentice experienced a large being, usually a huge, magic bear that came and devoured him. Later he woke up, was reborn, and experienced himself fleeing. He then became a different person with the power to commune with his helping spirits.

These special shaman stones can still be found out in the countryside of Greenland in remote and inaccessible areas. They often have a shallow depression and are as smooth as silk after being used for generations.

As mentioned, the intention was to acquire as large an arsenal of helping spirits – toornat – as possible and, in addition – a toornaarsuk – a more personal helping spirit. This is often seen illustrated on e.g. the harpoon throwing stick, where a small being

with two "arms" and the lower body of a seal is explained as a toornaarsuk-figure.

The drum was the most important tool involved in making contact with toornat – the helping spirits. Spells and magic songs were also used during the séance.

Anyone could use amulets, but they were used by the shaman in particular when he needed extra protection when he made contact with the spirits.

When the training was deemed to be complete, an initiation ceremony, witnessed by the settlement took place and when it was over and acknowledged, a new shaman was ready.

THE WINTER HOUSE

When it is bitterly cold and snowstorms rage, you need adequate protection against the elements if you are to survive at Greenlandic latitudes. This is why the Greenlanders' traditional winter house was built with thick walls of stone and turf, to ensure survival through the winter.

The house could be of a considerable size, being about 10-15 metres long and 4-5 metres wide, depending on how many people it was intended for. The walls were built of alternate layers of stone and grass turf. Struts made of driftwood were raised in the middle to support the eaves. These were in turn covered by branches and pieces of split driftwood, upon which large pieces of grass turf were laid with the grass-side down. Finally, it was all covered with

an old skin from a women's boat (umiaq). And soon the snow covered everything!

The entrance was a long, narrow, sunken passage-way about 6-8 metres long. Its low position helped to keep the cold out of the house. The house usually had three small windows, one at each end with a smaller window above the passage. They were made of seal intestines which had been cut open lengthwise and sewed together. Naturally, you could not see through them, but they did allow a certain amount of light in. Above the entrance there was also a smoke hole which could be opened and closed as required. The floor was covered with thin, flat stones and there were seal skins on the wall.

In his book "The Umiak Expedition to East Green-land" Gustav Holm writes about a house of the size in question, lived in by 38 people from 8 different groups varying from 1 to 10 persons. If you think about how many square metres there were for each person, it is not surprising that they looked forward to the summer and the freedom of living in smaller groups in tents.

The house consisted of one large room. Sealskins were hung up as partitions for the different groups and a long sleeping platform ran along the back of the house.

According to Gustav Holm, a sleeping platform

measuring just one and a half metres could accommodate a whole family of husband, two wives and six children. The sleeping platform by the window was used by young, unmarried men or the few guests that turned up during the winter.

By the side of its sleeping platform, each family had an oil lamp. It functioned as lighting, heating and cooking stove. There was probably a good temperature in the winter house, generated by the heat from the large number of people and the burning, soapstone oil lamps. A bucket of water was kept next to the oil lamp. Stored under the sleeping platform were skins, tools and supplies, as well as a blubber pot, meat trays and the urine pot.

During the winter storms, people were often forced to spend many days indoors and the time was spent repairing/manufacturing tools and clothing, telling stories and reminiscing about the summer's hunting trips and visits.

Towards the end of March and the beginning of April, the time came to move back into the summer tents. The roof of the winter house was taken off, so that the wind and weather could take care of the airing and spring cleaning. When autumn approached once more, it was decided which family groups would spend the winter together. You did not necessarily move into the same house again. You might build in another place or simply move in somewhere else.

You can often find the ruins of these houses if you are out in the countryside. The remains of the thick walls are often found in an especially green spot, always situated close to the sea.

Turf houses were still being built far into the last century, although now in a more modern form with wooden floors and walls, and equipped with stoves and perhaps more rooms.

THE SOAP-STONE LAMP

In a country where the winters are cold, dark and long, a small source of heat has immense significance.

Greenland's soapstone lamp or blubber lamp as it is also called has many functions – as a light source, a heat source and as a "stove" for the cooking pot. It was carved out of the soft soapstone in many different sizes depending on the intended use.

The fuel in the lamp was blubber, derived primarily from seals, but also from other marine mammals.

In its most well-known form, the half-moon shaped lamp, the blubber was placed at the back of the lamp and the oil flowed slowly down towards the front to a long wick of dried moss, where it burned evenly with a small flame. A small stick was used to keep the flame constantly regulated so that it burned evenly along the edge, making sure fuel was not wasted. The life-giving flame had to be looked after and if the flame died, the fire drill was the most usual method of starting a new fire.

In the winter house, where the sleeping platform along the back wall was separated into sections by a skin curtain, each family had its own lamp burning in front of its own space. One of the most important tasks of a hunter's wife was to keep the lamp burning evenly, so it didn't smoke and gave out most light and heat.

Many of the larger lamps were equipped with a transverse ridge that kept the blubber in place at the back of the lamp. A soap-stone lamp obviously became very hot

when it was used and it had to be placed on an insulated base, often a large, flat stone, or – later – a fine, three legged lamp stand made of wood, often with a depression at the bottom into which excess oil from the blubber could run.

Soap stone lamps have taken on different forms and functions with the various Inuit cultures that have migrated to Greenland over the past. From large, half-moon shaped lamps about 30-40 cm across with room for a lot of blubber used under large, soapstone cooking pots, to small, round lamps where the wick was placed against a small stone cone in the middle.

For thousands of years the weak light from a small soapstone lamp was the only lighting in the small turf huts in winter. Many stories and legends have been told in its light and many beautiful tools and skin garments have been produced.

The soapstone lamp has long since fallen in to disuse, but it is still found in many homes in Greenland as a symbol of the warmth and light that has helped Inuit cultures through many long, dark, cold winters.

WATER POTS FROM EAST GREENLAND

Everybody needs water – especially a diet that consists of meat and fat requires lots of cold, fresh water. When you have the world's purest and most delicious water within reach, it will surely only heighten your enjoyment if the water is served in a beautifully decorated container. This must have been the philosophy of the people of East Greenland, whose water pots are an expression of Greenlandic handicraft at its most beautiful. The famous water pots of East Greenland, richly decorated with beautifully fashioned figures, are the epitome of superb Greenlandic handcraft. The pots are made as ordinary, everyday utensils with elements from nature and mythology worked in.

The water pots are made in the same way as barrels, i.e. a series of narrow, flat, wooden slats carved in driftwood are fitted together with precision. The bottom of the barrel fits into grooves near the end of the slats. The slats are drawn together at the top with bone mounts and riveted with small wooden pegs. Decorations of seals, whales and mythological

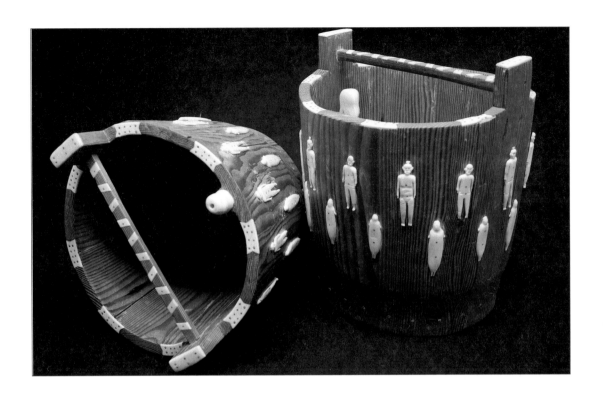

figures are riveted onto the sides of the pots. A lump of ice is put into the pot, where it slowly melts. Sometimes, as a special refinement, one of the slats can be hollowed out and finished with a hollow bone tip for drinking – like a built-in drinking straw. It makes it easier to take a drink without removing the lump of ice. Alternatively, a long-handled ladle can be used.

The same technique was used to make the slightly larger urine pots, which were more simply made and usually not decorated. They had their place under the bed and the contents were used to wash hair and to tan hides.

These pots were already being made when Gustav Holm came to Ammassalik in 1884, but it is not known how the people of East Greenland learned the technique. It is probable that the East Greenlanders, with their ability to assimilate new tools and techniques, learned the art from seeing barrels used to store oil in their sporadic contact to southernmost Greenland. It is just as probable that they found barrels of different sizes washed up along the coast, debris from whaling ships wrecked over centuries in the ice along the coast. East Greenland has always been favoured with plenty of driftwood and many exciting items have washed ashore to be carefully and parsimoniously utilised by the local people.

The craftsmen of East Greenland still make these beautiful water pots in a very fine quality.

AMAAT

Amaat is the female counterpart to the men's anorak. It was characterised by the large hood and the very wide shoulders, as well as its decoration. The decoration usually consisted of white leather strips sewn into the seams, but later on, glass beads were also used. The word "amaat" could have been one of the few Inuit words to become internationally known, like "anorak" and "kayak". It was an extremely practical item of clothing, which fulfilled several purposes: it was the outer garment for a mother, a cradle for the baby and a kind of rucksack.

An amaat had to keep the mother and the baby warm – vital in an Arctic climate. By lying in the hood up against its mother's back, the baby received comfort and warmth, and was soothed by the movements of its mother, as she went about her daily work. It was a well thought-out and practical garment for a no-

Jette Bang/ © Arktisk Institut

madic people. Even new-born babies could be carried in the amaat. Caribou skin or moss was used for diapers.

The wide shoulders meant the baby could easily be pulled round to the breast without being exposed to the cold. The baby was carried in the amaat for 2 to 3 years. A strap fastened to the front of the garment was passed round the back and tied to the front. This prevented the collar from being pressed against the wearer's throat, and kept the baby upright and balanced.

The large hood enabled bigger babies to peek out and allowed the air to circulate, so the baby could breathe, even when it lay deep in the hood. Young girls who looked after small brothers and sisters could also wear an amaat.

The women's clothing was made of the same materials as the men's, for the most part sealskin prepared in different ways. During the winter, an undergarment was worn against the skin and over it, an outer garment with the hair facing inwards. The air trapped between the two layers of skin insulated very well against the cold. The garment's hem dipped at the back and the front, with longer snips on the women's garment.

All measurements for a new garment were taken by eye and the pattern was so familiar that it could be cut freehand. The skin was cut from the meat side

with an ulu (women's knife) taking care not to damage the hairs.

An amaat made of white cotton is part of the national costume of East Greenland today. With its simple and beautiful appearance, it is very different from the well-known colourful costumes of West Greenland.

Older finds of Greenlandic garments show that the garments have not undergone significant changes right up to present times. The optimal design for Arctic life had been found.

It is characteristic that the design of the garments has not changed very much, despite the introduction of guns and new fishing and hunting methods. It is just as characteristic, that the first explorers in the Arctic only became successful, when they started to use Eskimo garments and forms of travel.

THE NATIONAL COSTUME

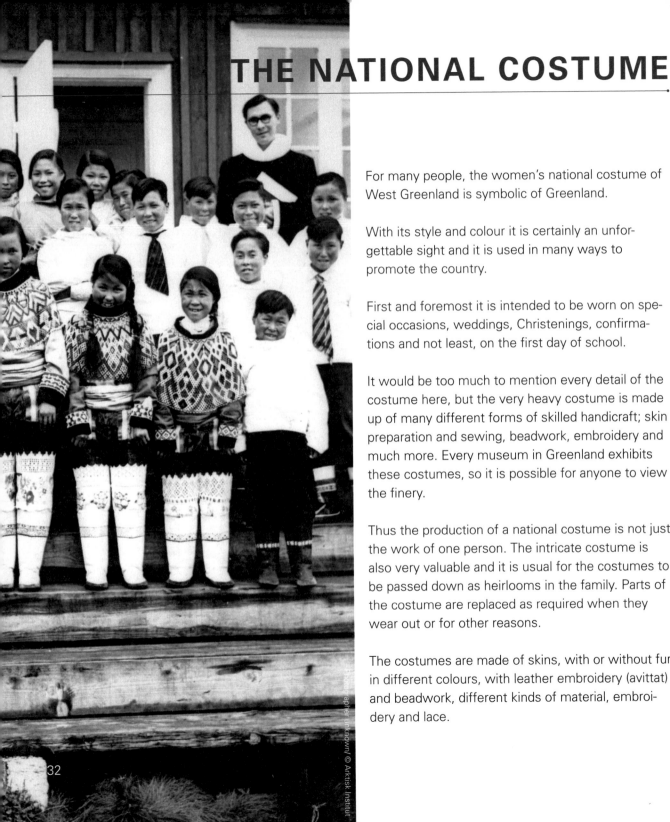

For many people, the women's national costume of West Greenland is symbolic of Greenland.

With its style and colour it is certainly an unforgettable sight and it is used in many ways to promote the country.

First and foremost it is intended to be worn on special occasions, weddings, Christenings, confirmations and not least, on the first day of school.

It would be too much to mention every detail of the costume here, but the very heavy costume is made up of many different forms of skilled handicraft; skin preparation and sewing, beadwork, embroidery and much more. Every museum in Greenland exhibits these costumes, so it is possible for anyone to view the finery.

Thus the production of a national costume is not just the work of one person. The intricate costume is also very valuable and it is usual for the costumes to be passed down as heirlooms in the family. Parts of the costume are replaced as required when they wear out or for other reasons.

The costumes are made of skins, with or without fur, in different colours, with leather embroidery (avittat) and beadwork, different kinds of material, embroidery and lace.

Photographer unknown/ © Arktisk Institut

The West Greenland costume developed over a couple of centuries before arriving at its present, probably almost final form. From a fragile start, when glass beads first became available, the impressive and heavy collar developed from a few rows of beads to the now well-known top weighing up to 1½ kilos. The patterns in the bead collar are usually symmetrical, but roses and green leaves also occur.

New fabrics and other exciting things were added to the costume, as they became available.

Enthusiasm for the costume of West Greenland should not make us forget the other two national costumes: the Thule costume and the costume from East Greenland. They are completely different in appearance, not nearly as decorative, but definitely just as beautiful. They have their own style and originality and reflect a separate culture and nature.

The men's national dress is different, more modest but naturally also elegant. It consists of a white anorak, where the cut varies from district to district, together with dark trousers and "kamiks" (seal skin boots).

ULU – THE WOMAN'S KNIFE

Throughout history, the most important tools of the Inuit were without any doubt the knife and the needle. Knives were used for cutting up the animals they caught and for preparing the skins, and needles were used for sewing clothing and footwear able to withstand the extreme climate of the Inuit habitat. These are tools that still have an important place in modern Greenland. The blades of the knives were fashioned out of stone, whilst the needles were made from filed splinters of bone.

Metal and metal tools were therefore amongst the most sought-after trading items during the first contact with Europeans.

The "ulu", the crescent-shaped knife, is an example of a tool where the original form was inevitably determined by its function. This is why the ulu has been invented by many cultures independently of each other.

The ulu is known troughout the Eskimo region. It also appears in a similar form as a flint scraper from the Scandinavian Stone Age and as an ulu-like forerunner of the Greenlandic Stone Age cultures: a hewn rock without a handle, (a piece of skin was probably used to hold the stone, to protect the fingers).

Later on, the top of the blade was fitted with a handle of bone or wood. The piece of the handle attached to the knife was over time gradually lengthened allowing for a better control of the ulu. The ulu can still be found in almost every home in Greenland, where it is used not only for its original purpose, but also as a kind of universal tool. Today, it is used to cut the fine strips associated with leather decorations, avittat, seen on national costumes and purses etc., where tiny coloured leather strips are sewn into intricate geometrical patterns. It is also very useful for chopping parsley and nuts and is indispensable when serving such delicacies as mattak (whale blubber), dried meat and fish.

In Greenland, the woman's knife has developed into three different types. The West Greenlandic ulu has a pointed, oval blade with one bar. The Thule model has a more rounded blade and the bar, often made of brass, splits into two parts towards the blade. The ulu, or tsakkeq, from East Greenland is very different from the other two. The blade is square and there are two bars from the handle to the blade.

These designs show that in Thule and East Greenland people often produced their own blades, either by cutting them out of old saw blades or, as in East Greenland, by using the hoops from barrels washed up on the shore.

For some time now, it has been possible to buy factory-made blades in West Greenland.

It is still the women who are the primary users of the ulu, whilst it is the men who make them. There has never been a production of ready-made ulu in Greenland, although this is known from Canada and Alaska.

Use of the ulu can be seen everywhere in Greenland, either for flaying seals or in the local sewing workshops.

BEADS

Most people probably associate bead work in Greenland with the large bead collars which are so characteristic of the Greenlandic women's national costume. Beautiful, colourful and very heavy, they form a significant part of the costume. Beads have been used in Arctic regions for thousands of years, but the large bead collar has fairly recent origins, first taken into use at the beginning of the 1900's.

For thousands of years beads have been used in Eskimo cultures. Previously, many different materials were used to make the beads; stone, bones and teeth from small animals and small fish vertebra. Early beads were probably used as amulets. In East Greenland at least, it was believed that evil spirits could slip away through the small hole in the bead. The beads had many different shapes; round, oval or carved in the shape of animals. Archaeologists at a dig in the 1980's found no less than 632 beads in the remains of a small house in Jameson Land in Northeast Greenland – the largest find of its kind in Greenland.

These beads were from about 1800 and the members of the small family that lived here must have been bead experts, manufacturing beads both for their own use and for trade with others.

The beads were mainly animal figures, mostly seals, but also birds and bears were found in the collection. The other beads were various tear-formed beads and tooth beads, i.e. small polished teeth from seals, foxes and other animals. They were probably used both for necklaces and hair decoration, or they were sewn onto clothing as decoration or used as amulets.

Glass beads were brought to Greenland in the 1600's by Dutch sailors on whaling expeditions in Greenlandic waters. The first glass beads were very large and were sewn onto costumes in short rows as decoration. At the end of the 1700's the first small glass beads, as we know them today, arrived in Greenland. They quickly became just as popular here, as everywhere else in the world, where they were introduced. Glass beads, and needles were highly prized by the Greenlanders.

In the beginning, the beads were used sparingly on the national costume. But as the beads became more widely available and the Greenlanders' skill in using them increased, so did the size of the bead collar, reflecting the economic means of the owner and thereby becoming a status symbol. Bead collars weigh about one kilo.

It was traditional in East Greenland to use vertebra from the capelin, a small member of the trout family, as beads. They were small, about one millimetre in diameter and they were natural-coloured, coloured with blood or coloured with soot from an oil lamp. The small glass beads were especially popular here.

The use of beads to decorate the national costume of East Greenland is less extravagant than in West Greenland. In West Greenland all the colours are used, whereas in East Greenland beads of white, blue and red are predominant.

The use of bone beads was widespread in East Greenland. If you take a look at the many objects collected by Gustav Holm when he came to East Greenland in 1883-84, you will see the many uses of bone beads; as earrings, on eye-shades, on throwing boards and on kayak-parts, on bracelets, necklaces and amulet-straps. There were, and are, countless ways to use the beads.

All over Greenland, there is still an abundant pro-duction of traditionally-inspired trinkets and orna-ments using beads made of bone, ivory and glass.

AVITTAT – LEATHER EMBROIDERY

One of the finest of Greenland's handicrafts is the many-coloured leather embroidery – avittat – which is sewn in a narrow strip on the skin pants of the national costume. It is also part of the decoration on kamiks and is used as a border on bags, purses and other items.

The embroidery consists of tiny, millimetre-long, coloured pieces of thin leather that are sewn onto a background of dyed, usually white, skin. The tiny pieces of leather, which may be down to one millimetre in length and width, are sewn individually in intricate patterns with fine stitches.

The process is like this: a long, thin strip of leather is fastened with stitches at one end, the strip is cut and the next end is sewn in place. The whole process is then repeated with another colour. One exception however, is on the women's pants where the decoration on the thighs is sewn on from the back, so that the stitches can't be seen from the front. The leather used here is a little thicker than usual for leather embroidery because there has to be room for needle and thread at the edge of the work.

Previously, thread made of reindeer sinews was used, but nowadays a fine sewing thread is used instead. The sinew thread could be split into very fine strands that were moistened and rolled so they became completely smooth.

The leather pieces used to form the patterns were previously dyed with plant dyes but later ready-made lacquers were used.

As with so many other skilled handicrafts, full consensus does not exist as to which methods or measurements are best, although some swear by tiny squares, whilst other believe this makes patterning more difficult. The dye method is also a subject with many variations, but whatever the choice, it is always beautiful and an expression of Greenlandic handicraft of the highest calibre.

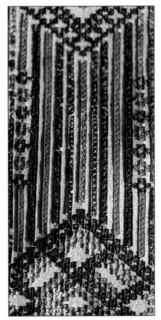

THE KAYAK

"The kayak is undoubtedly the most outstanding, one-man vessel ever made," the Norwegian polar explorer Fridtjof Nansen wrote after spending a winter in Greenland in 1888-89.

Together with the women's boat (umiaq) and the dog sled the kayak was an important craft for the survival and distribution of the Inuit from Siberia to the East coast of Greenland.

The East Greenlandic kayak is the perfect vessel for hunting large marine mammals. Developed from the experience of generations and adapted to the hunting grounds of the Greenlandic Inuit, it is a testimony to the incredible ability to adapt to an Arctic environment.

The East Greenlandic kayak is distinct from the West Greenlandic kayak; it is usually longer and wider, adapted to hunting on the open sea.

The form of the kayak varies in Greenland, depending on the prevailing wind-, water- and weather conditions at the intended place of use. But the fundamental principle is the same; the kayak is built, tailored to fit the user so as to achieve perfect balance and fit. It is therefore not a good idea to borrow someone else's kayak.

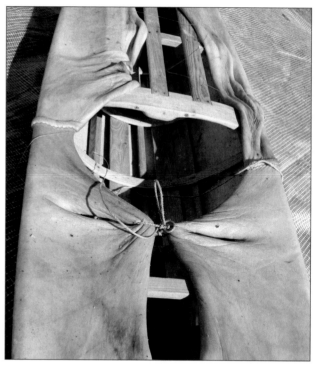

A well-equipped kayak includes a large number of weapons or hunting tools designed for the catch of the prey most common to the area.

The kayak's success as a seagoing vessel was not only due to the construction as such, but also to the development of suitable clothing.

Here, as in every other aspect of life in traditional Greenland, the well-being of the hunter and of the whole family depended on the seamstress skills of the hunter's wife. She mastered the art of preparing the skins and making them into warm functional clothing, protecting the family against climate ex-tremes to secure their survival. A good hunter could have 2 wives, because there were so many skins to be taken care of.

Today the kayak has only limited use for hunting pur-poses, but is used in connection with the hunting of narwhales, shy animals, which need to be har-pooned in order not to sink, before the riffle is used. Modern kayaks have the same construction as the traditional kayak, although the materials have changed from sealskin to painted linen or glass fibre. Hooks are moulded into the glass fibre for attaching the harpoon and hunting bladder.

The kayak has experienced a renaissance as a sports craft. Many towns have annual kayaking competitions to maintain the knowledge and skills of the kayak hunter. The kayaks used here are the same as the originals.

TUILIK – THE KAYAK SPRAYSUIT

Many people associate the kayak of Greenland with skilful kayakers, making difficult rolls and coming up again after capsizing.

In order to achieve this astonishing exercise, the kayaker needs clothing that makes him one with his craft.

It was to this end that the tuilik was developed. It is a suit shaped like a long anorak, reaching down to the knees of a standing kayaker. It is made of soft sealskin, from which the hair has been removed and the double seams are sewn with fine, small stitches. It is rubbed with seal blubber oil to make it softer and to make it waterproof.

The tuilik has drawstrings at the wrists and round the face, to seal the suit tight to the body. There is also a drawstring along the bottom edge, for tightening around the cockpit coaming. When all the drawstrings have been tightened and tied, the kayaker is one with his craft and is able to roll round in the water and contend with splashing waves without water getting into the kayak. The kayak is therefore suitable for use in rough seas. The air trapped within the suit provides floatation and insulation against the cold. The "skirt" is long

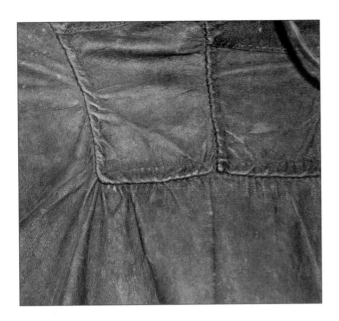 

enough, to allow the kayaker to push himself some centimetres out of the kayak without spoiling the waterproof seal. This detail can be critical if the kayak capsizes and is difficult to right again.

Over the years, there has been a tendency towards shorter tuiliks and this has cost many kayakers their lives.

The writer H.C. Petersen wrote in his book "Skin Boats of Greenland" about this unfortunate development: In an interview with his friend Peter Petrussen, Peter recounts how he, as a young kayaker, was embarrassed by the skin suit his mother had made for him. – It looked too much like a girl's dress,

he said, and he didn't like to walk through the village wearing it.

Nevertheless, one day Petrussen wore it in his kayak. He capsized and even though he had never been taught how to right his kayak, he was able to push himself up out of the kayak ring without breaking the "seal", thanks to the long skin suit. He was able to get his head above water and call for help. – In my thoughts I thanked my mother. She was right. I would probably have drowned, if I had worn the modern, shorter version.

Nowadays, people who practice the sport of kayaking still use the tuilik, but there are more

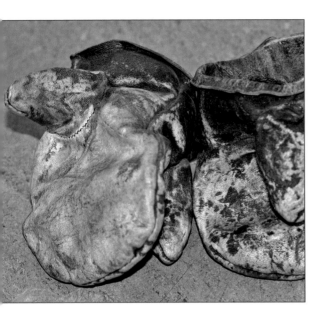

modern versions made of neoprene and other
artificial materials.

In its original version, made of softened sealskin
with carved toggles on the ends of the drawstrings,
the tuilik is a beautiful example of the cultural history
of Greenland that is still in use today.

THE HARPOON

While modern technology has replaced many of the Greenlanders' traditional hunting tools, the use of the finest tool – the harpoon – persists in present times.

At first sight the harpoon may seem simple and un-complicated, but a closer look proves that this tool has the ultimate design for hunting large sea ani-mals. The harpoon, made out of available materials, has been perfected under the influence of genera-tions and modified according to the topography of the area where the Inuit lived.

A shaft mounted with a tip is known from other an-cient hunting cultures, but to elongate this tool with a fore shaft and a loose head is a technique that has only been developed by the Inuit.

A fully equipped kayak has a minimum of four hunting tools, various weapons for throwing (harpoons), weapons for thrusting (lances) fixed to the deck as well as a number of knives and other pointed weapons.

All types of harpoon can be roughly described as two-metre long wooden shafts with a moveable fore shaft of about 20 cm – usually made of walrus or narwhal tusk – and a harpoon head. This is usually made of sperm whale tusk and fitted with a metal blade. Usually, a throwing board of about half a metre is used to accelerate the cast.

A 15-20 metre long line made of strips of bearded seal skin is fastened to the harpoon head. The line is neatly coiled on top of the kayak in front of the hunter and the end of the line is attached to a float placed on the kayak behind the hunter.

There are two ingenious mechanisms in the con-struction. First, there is the loose fore shaft, which prevents the harpoon shaft from breaking during the animal's violent movements in the water. Second, there is the loose head, which is connected to the float by a line. The shaft with the loose fore shaft de-taches from the head after being thrust into the ani-mal and can be picked out of the water later.

The harpoon head, which is constructed so that it ro-tates inside the animal, is now fixed in place. The animal pulls the float after itself and is followed and killed by the hunter. The float prevents the animal from diving or sinking so that it is lost.

It takes a tough mixture of good balance and fast reactions to fire this "three stage rocket" from a bobbing kayak in that short moment the animal is within range.

One hand is used to paddle and steer the kayak and the other is used to throw the heavy, powerful har-poon. The throwing board is held in the mouth after the throw and an intense watch is kept to see if the animal has been hit, all the while keeping the kayak in balance. If the hunter hits his prey, the line and float must be freed and thrown into the air at the right moment. Misjudgement or hesitation could have fatal consequences for an inexperienced hunter. No wonder this is an art that must be learned in childhood in order to be mastered perfectly.

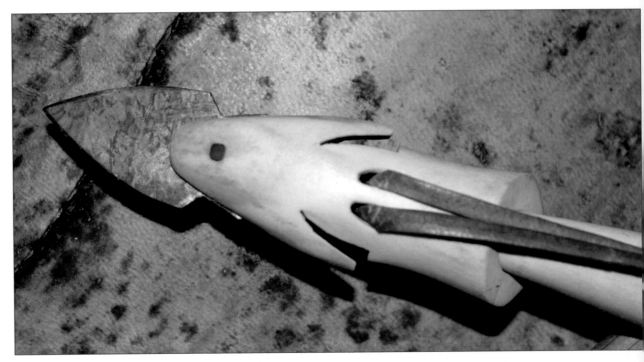

THROWING BOARD

The throwing board, or "norsaq" in Greenlandic, is not exclusively an Eskimo invention. It has existed in almost all hunting cultures and is a much older invention than the bow and arrow.

The throwing board is a powerful instrument that functions as an extension of the arm, enabling the weapon, a spear or harpoon, to be thrown much further and with more force than would otherwise be possible.

However, this is not its only function. The throwing board also ensures that the hunter's grasp on the harpoon is the same every time and that the point of balance is the same for each throw. The throwing board is held in the hand with the underside uppermost, so that the harpoon rests in a groove in the board.

The technique is of particular importance to the Greenlandic hunter in his kayak close to the water's surface, enabling him to throw the harpoon and secure his catch. The throwing board has actually attained a high

William Thalbitzer/ © Arktisk Institut

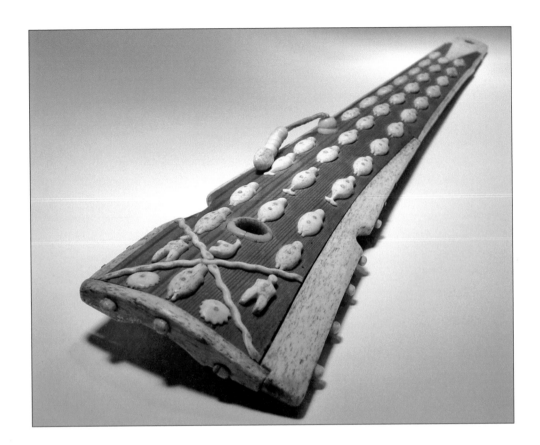

degree of technical development in Greenland and it is a very practical and often beautifully decorated tool.

Apart from being used as a hunting tool, the throwing board can also be used in tricky situations. The Greenlandic hunter has many ways to right his kayak after capsizing. One of these is to take hold of the throwing board and use it as a small paddle.

The throwing board is found in many forms, depending on local materials and traditions, but usually it is a piece of wood about 45-60 cm long, with a lengthwise groove on the underside in which the spear or harpoon rests. It is slightly curved and it is widest at the front where there are usually grips for the thumb and index finger and it narrows towards the back.

The board has two holes. The front hole is used only for fastening the throwing board to a bone peg on the harpoon when it is not in use. The back hole fits a spur on the harpoon, and it is here the transfer of force takes place. Fastening the throwing board with two holes is a technique which is only found in

Greenland. The wood is often too weak to withstand the violent effect of the transfer of force and this part of the throwing board is therefore often reinforced or replaced by a piece of bone.

To avoid having too many different implements lying on the deck of the kayak, a throwing board is often adapted for use with various weapons. Sometimes the throwing board is fitted with a small leather strap and a bone bead so that it can be fastened to the deck of the kayak when it is not in use.

In East Greenland in particular, where the throwing boards are often longer and narrower than the boards found on the West Coast, they are richly decorated with bone edges and studded with flat, embossed figures of game carved in narwhal or walrus tusk. The motifs are often seals, bears, whales and humans and, in the age before the introduction of Christianity, also spiritual beings, especially the little Tornaarsuk figure. Its purpose is not fully understood, but it is thought to have been an important helping spirit for the Greenlandic shaman's travels to the spiritual world.

The throwing board is still used in those parts of Greenland where the kayak and the harpoon are used for hunting and use of the harpoon is a discipline which is still practiced in kayak clubs in Greenland.

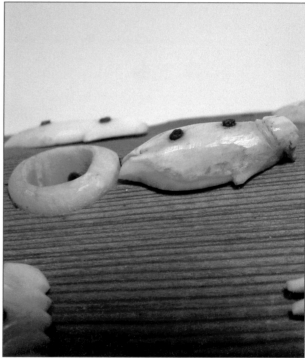

THE KAYAK KNIFE

A well-equipped kayak included a large number of weapons or hunting tools designed to catch precisely those animals that were prevalent in the hunting area. The weapons could be divided into two groups. Throwing weapons, which were various harpoon types used to catch the animal and stabbing weapons, consisting of lances and knives with which to kill the animal.

The kayak knife, or short lance, was one of the stabbing weapons. As the name implies, there was also a long lance, which was a weapon useful for catching swimming animals.

The design of the kayak knife varied according to its district of origin. Some were rather too long to be called knives.

The kayak knife, in all its simplicity, consisted of an oval wooden shaft about 1 metre long, with a 20-30 cm keenly sharpened iron tip fixed by a bone ring to the shaft. To go with the knife – or lance – there was

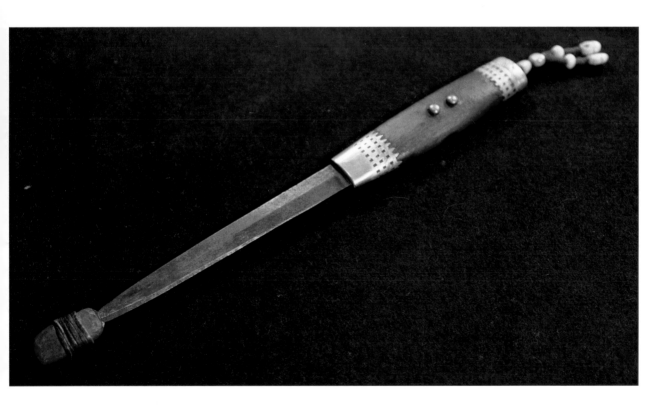

also a wooden scabbard, covering about one third of the tip.

The scabbard was attached to the kayak to protect both the tip of the knife as well as the kayak. Because of its length, the lance could not be used as a knife, so there was also a shorter version, about half as long and with a tip of 10 cm.

The purpose of these smaller weapons was to kill animals that were potentially dangerous if they got close to the kayak, where the long lance was not easily used.

The clever hunter could sometimes avoid using the float when he caught small seals, simply by pulling the animal to the kayak by the harpoon line and killing the animal with the kayak knife.

In East Greenland, a small kayak knife was used for the same purpose, but it was the size of a normal knife, about 30 - 40 cm. It was often beautifully decorated, which is customary for the toolmakers of East Greenland. The blade could be made of narwhal tusk, honed to a point, very sharp and absolutely strong enough to kill a small seal.

There was a 10-cm, 2-part strop on the handle, decorated with bone beads. The knife was placed under the strap on the deck of the kayak and the idea of the strops with the beads was that the knife was easy to pull out from under the strap with the strops held between the three middle fingers.

This knife is still in production although not for its original purpose. It is now used as a souvenir or as a paper knife, where it represents a beautiful example of East Greenland craftsmanship and is testimony to an ancient and noble hunting culture.

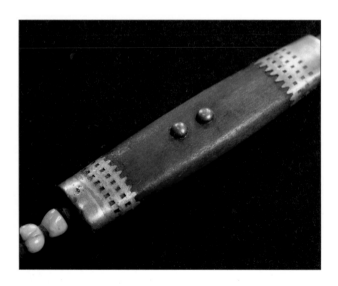

One of the smaller weapons is the bird arrow, a throwing weapon for catching birds on the water or in low flight. It can be hard to hit a seal from a kayak, but even harder to hit a small bird, bobbing up and down on the water; this requires a specially-designed hunting tool.

The bird arrow is characterised by three, occasionally four, forward-pointing bone prongs that are placed in a ring around the middle of the shaft. The bone prongs have barbs and in several ways they resemble a fishing spear.

They are usually made of caribou antler, which is readily available in most of the country and is a strong material that is easy to work with. The angle between the shaft and the bone points is important. If the angle is too wide the points will break off. But if it is too narrow it will be difficult to fix the bird. Most hunters use the width of three fingers as a measure for the distance between shaft and point.

The idea is that should the tip of the bird arrow miss, one of the three prongs on the "spear" could hit the mark instead. This means that the weapon has a "spread" that could be compared to the effect of a shotgun versus a rifle.

The tip was traditionally fashioned out of bone with a single barb. Later on, an iron rod was used, where

the end was sharpened and given one or more barbs.

The tip is anchored directly into the shaft and fastened with binding. At the end there is a small bone knob which fits into the throwing board. The relatively light bird arrow can be thrown for a con-siderably longer distance than the heavy harpoon used for hunting seals. The bird arrow has also been used to catch small seals.

The shaft of the bird arrow is 120 - 150 cm long, but it is not evenly thick along the whole length.

The three thickest parts are 1) the front of the shaft

where the tip is inserted in a hole, 2) the middle, where the three bone points are mounted, and 3) the end of the shaft where the bone knob for the throwing board is mounted.

The bird arrow, which is a unique example of kayak technology, quickly fell into disuse when the shot-gun became more widespread.

UMIAQ – THE WOMEN'S BOAT

The umiaq is the Inuit's journey and family boat and it is probably as old as the Inuit culture itself.

Inuit migration from the remote regions of Siberia to East Greenland would have been unthinkable without the umiaq. The umiaq is known throughout the region and the word for the boat is similar everywhere in the Arctic where the inuits reside. However, the form and purpose varies from the small umiaqs in Alaska, that are used for hunting larger whales, to the wider, more spacious transport boats used in Greenland.

It was called the women's boat, as it was the women who rowed the boat, whilst the men sailed alongside in their kayaks. Loaded as it was with household implements, children and perhaps dogs, summer tent etc., it carried the worldly possessions of the whole family. There were usually four women rowing and, to some extent, a sail was used for propulsion.

The umiaq was used for summer transportation and it was indispensable for Greenlanders. In this large, extensive country with deep fjords and countless islands in skerries, it was necessary then, as now, with transportation that could bring the whole family across long distances. People met at the hunting grounds or at the big summer gatherings. Family visits and summer gatherings, where you met new people, exchanged news and made agreements for the coming year, were events that were looked forward to, after the long winter isolation.

The families sailed together to gather provisions. The big spring seal migration at the outer islands where meat was dried, fishing for capelin and later Arctic char and the caribou hunt were all part of the rhythm of the season.

The boats returned home before the advent of autumn's dangerous, thin ice, heavily laden with provisions for the long winter. Nevertheless, a tear or hole in the boat's skin was not necessarily fatal. A

piece of blubber was pushed into the hole and when the boat came ashore, it could easily be repaired with the needle and sinew thread that was always stowed at the top of the baggage.

Although the women's boat in Greenland was primarily a cargo vessel capable of carrying many kilos, it was a very light construction that could be carried over land or up onto ice flows, if the ice suddenly blocked the way.

It was used for night shelter during the many days' journey to the summer places. It was carried ashore and turned upside down. Supported by a small stick on one side it quickly provided good shelter for the night. The same naturally applied, if the weather turned bad – storm or rain – on the way. It was probably a beautiful sight in the summer night, al-

most like Chinese lanterns on the beach, with light shining through the skin of the umiaq and the ribs of the boat like a dark, regular pattern against the golden skin.

The oldest known umiaq in Greenland and the oldest in the world, is the 500-year old umiaq, which was found at the end of the 1940's in northernmost East Greenland, in Pearyland by polar explorer Eigil Knuth. The boat is also the longest ever to be found in Greenland, with a length of 11 metres, it is narrower than the umiaqs that were usually used in Greenland and resembles more those used in Alaska for whale hunting. Whether it had made the journey from Alaska to East Greenland is obviously not known, but it is quite possible.

A copy of the old boat was made at the Viking Ship Museum in Roskilde in 1980. Elderly Greenlanders from the Nanortalik region in South Greenland came to Roskilde to build the boat.

The umiaq was in use up to 40 - 50 years ago and has now been replaced by boats with motors, so it is becoming increasingly difficult to find people with the skill to build umiaqs.

"Give me winter, give me dogs – you can keep the rest," said the famous polar explorer Knud Rasmussen. Throughout a long life, he had used dog sleds on his famous expeditions in Greenland, Canada and Alaska. These were the expeditions which were immortalised in his series of books, where the reader feels he has a front row seat as the dog sled fights its way through the ice and snow-covered landscape. Knud Rasmussen understood the importance of the dogs' efforts for the success of an expedition. In his books, the polar explorer always underlines his relationship to the sled dogs. He tells of the hierarchy within the group so intimately, that a whole four-legged family suddenly comes to life on the page.

And the command "iip, iip" fortunately still sounds from the hunters, as they swing their whips in front of the teams of dogs speeding across snow-covered landscapes or bright ice.

Snow mobiles are certainly giving this ancient form of Arctic transportation increasing competition. But dog sled tracks are not so easily wiped out by progress. The dog sled is still a fundamental part of a hunter's way of life. And many hunters earn a welcome supplement to their income by taking tourists for rides – a phenomenon which more than any other links dog sledding with pictures of Greenland.

Today, the dog sled is used mainly for hunting, social trips and for transportation to and from the sea ice to fish for Greenland halibut. Hunting trips are primarily aimed at seals, which are caught in nets, whilst in the spring they are shot as they sun themselves on the ice. Moreover, long dog sled trips to hunt for polar bears are common in North and East Greenland, where these Arctic kings are most prevalent.

With one exception, the dog sled has been a part of

all Inuit cultures. Throughout time, the dog sled has been found in many different versions. Some of them were quite primitive, but like the kayak, the dog sled has achieved a high technological standard over the centuries, making it ideal for transportation in Arctic regions.

The sleds are made of pieces of wood lashed together, avoiding the use of nails where possible. This means that the sleds can writhe and twist in uneven terrain and avoid being damaged by the inevitable jolts and bumps of dog sledding. Modern techniques have of course also made their mark. Nylon rope is usually used for the lashings and the runners are made of iron or plastic. Like the kayak, the dog sled is precisely fashioned to suit the terrain in which it is to be used. This explains why there are three different types of sled in Greenland:

The Thule sled, absolutely the longest of the three, is used primarily for sledding with heavy loads on sea ice. Since it is often necessary to cross cracks in the ice, a long sled is most suitable.

In the rest of Northwest Greenland – i.e. north of Sisimiut – sledding is done both on ice and overland. The sleds are therefore shorter and better suited to mixed terrain.

And finally, there is the dog sled from East Greenland which, until the turn of the previous century was quite a small sled, used only for short trips and for transportation of kayaks or umiaqs (women's boats) to the edge of the ice. Because of large snow masses and hilly terrain, it was also only used for short overland trips. However, after the French polar researcher Paul-Emile Victor's visit to East Greenland in the 1930's, the dog sled of East Greenland changed to the model we see today. It is somewhat larger, but still a light sled with wide runners, making it eminently suitable for regions with heavy snowfall. Victor's sled was inspired by the type of sled used by Nansen when he crossed the inland ice. It is unique amongst the sleds of Greenland in that it is equipped with a strong, metal footbrake to facilitate sledding in the hilly terrain.

The number of dogs and the way in which the team is arranged varies with the different types of sled.

The big Thule sleds originally had the largest teams whilst the small, traditional sleds of East Greenland used fewer dogs. But with the development of the East Greenland dog sled, the dog teams are now almost the same size in East and West Greenland.

Furthermore, in the Thule region the traces are very long, with the most obedient dog having an even longer trace, so that it can run in front, taking on the important role of leader.

In Northwest Greenland the traces are all the same length and, like the Thule region, the dogs run in a fan formation.

However, the heavy snowfall in East Greenland makes it necessary for the dogs' traces to be of different lengths. The dogs run more side by side with a lead dog at the head. In this way, the front dogs tread a more accessible path through the high snow, which makes it easier for the other dogs.

The shooting screen first came into use in the middle of the 1800's and was a new addition to the Greenlandic kayak.

Throughout its 1000-year development, the kayak had otherwise been fine-tuned to perfection for use as a vessel for hunting marine mammals, but the introduction of the rifle brought changes to the selection of tools required for hunting from the kayak.

The shooting screen is a piece of white material, about 65-80 cm in width (a little wider than a kayak) and about 30-40 cm high. It is stretched over a frame that is fastened to the front end of the kayak. A couple of pockets are sewn along the bottom and these are weighted with stones or lead weights, to keep the screen tight along both sides of the kayak.

The hunter hides himself behind this "curtain" and prepares to shoot as he slowly approaches his prey. The stalked animal perceives this camouflage screen as being a small iceberg.

The screen does not hide the hunter completely, since he has to look over the top of the screen, so he must wear light-coloured clothing.

Consequently, a white anorak and cap are part of his outfit. Usually the screen is rolled up during the trip and is not unfurled until the hunter approaches the hunting ground.

The life of the hunter obviously became easier with the advent of the rifle, with its longer range and greater precision. There are, however, also draw-

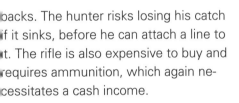

backs. The hunter risks losing his catch if it sinks, before he can attach a line to it. The rifle is also expensive to buy and requires ammunition, which again necessitates a cash income.

It is thought that the hunting screen evolved from the screen that was used in the spring seal hunts at blowholes on the ice. Here, the screen was fastened to a small sled where the rifle was also fastened. The hunter would push the sled in front of him, hiding behind the screen as he sneaked up within shooting range of a seal basking in the sun by its blowhole. This technique required that the seal be hit by the first shot.

Otherwise, it would dive into the blowhole and be lost.

It is thought that both the hunting screen and the rifle bag, which was fastened to the kayak, were developed in the Disko Bay area in the middle of the 1800's, but for a long time they were local phenomena.

Curiously enough, it was not a hunter, but a printer who, for the first time in Greenlandic history, brought the story of the new hunting technique to the rest of the country. Printer Lars Møller from Nuuk was on a visit in North Greenland in the 1880's and it was here that he learned of the new devices. He acquired a set for himself and described them in detail in the Greenlandic news-paper, Atuagagdliutit.

Thanks to his efforts, use of the shooting screen became wide-spread in Greenland before the turn of the century.

EYE SHIELDS AND SHADES

The light is strong in Greenland, especially in the spring when the sun is high in the sky and is reflected by snow and ice. Anyone who has been to Greenland knows this. You protect yourself against the strong light with smart sunglasses and caps of all kinds.

It is imperative for a person who is forced to go out in the snow and ice to hunt for survival to protect his eyes. The hunters in Greenland developed equipment for this purpose, long before anyone had even heard of sunglasses.

Most people are probably familiar with snow goggles with their characteristic narrow slits. They are fine for people travelling on sleds in the spring, or for walking across the ice on seal hunts. The inside of the snow goggles is covered with soot to reduce glare even further.

75

Not so well-known perhaps, are the beautiful eye shades with their beautifully carved bone decorations. Eye shades were used by the hunter in his kayak, when he paddled through drifting ice. They offered good protection against the glare of the sun reflected from the ice and they afforded a wider field of vision than snow goggles.

Older photos from East Greenland depict kayakers with fine, hood-like headdresses made of beautiful white fox fur with the tail hanging down at the back and a shade made of wood.

Instead of the whole hood, the shade was often used on its own. The shade could just be a flat board or it could have a very wide edge which was folded down at the front.

Common to all of them is that they were usually richly decorated with colourings of reddish clay or soot. This background showed off the small bone carvings beautifully. The strap holding the shade in place on the head often had two or more bone beads.

The decorations were usually very carefully made and could depict naturalistic scenes of people and animals, but more often they were simply ovals, said to represent stylised seals.

Sometimes they were seen in a continuous row along the bone edges that complete the shade. Other decorations used for the edges were geometrical figures formed by longer or shorter sticks and wavy figures. On top of the shield or shade

there were often two sun signs or eyes, giving the shade the features of a face. These motifs can be found in many of the artefacts made by the people of Ammassalik and also by the Inuit of the Bering Straits.

A great deal of labour was undoubtedly required to produce these practical yet decorative objects, especially when you remember that they were made without modern, electric tools using only a knife, a bow drill and a file.

This handicraft expresses the epitome of the traditional skilful craftwork of the East Greenlanders.

LITERATURE

C. Buys & J. Oosten:
Braving the cold. Leiden University, Holland, 1996

Christopher Cunningham:
Building the Greenland Kayak.
McGraw-Hill Education, 2003

Jakob Danielsen:
A Hunter's Life in Olden Days. Atuakkiorfik, 2002

Merete Demant Jakobsen:
Shamanism. Berghahn Books, 1999

Erik Erngaard:
Greenland then and now. Lademann, 1972

Asger Jorn:
Folk Art in Greenland.
Verlag der Buchhandlung Walther Konig, 2001

Robert McGhee:
Ancient People of the Arctic.
www.ubcpress.ca, 2001

Jean Malaurie:
Call of the North.
Harry N. Abrams, Inc., Publishers, 2001

Jean Malaurie:
Ultima Thule. W.W. Norton & Co., 2003

Wendell H. Oswalt:
Eskimos and Explorers.
University of Nebraska Press, 1991

H.C. Petersen:
Skinboats of Greenland.
Nationalmuseet, Grønlands Nationalmuseum &
Vikingeskibsmuseet Roskilde, 1986

H.C. Petersen & Michael Hauser:
The drum song tradition in Greenland.
Atuagkat, 2006

www.culture.gl

Ole G. Jensen
The Culture of Greenland in Glimpses

© Ole G. Jensen & milik publishing, 2007

Translation into English: Maria Holm
Lay-out: Tegnestuen Tita
Printing: Nørhaven Book, Denmark
Photos by the author, if no one else is mentioned.

First edition, second printing

ISBN 978-87-91359-29-3

This book is also published in Greenlandic, Danish, German and French.
Most of the articles have been published in Air Greenland's in-flight magazine *Suluk*

All rights reserved.
No part of this publication, except brief extracts for the purpose of review, may be
reproduced without the written permission of the publisher.

www.milik.gl